Welcome to the laboratory of the world!

Water fills the oceans and seas . . . but did you know that there is water high in the sky, and in the air around you? It's easy to forget that it must be there—until you see it as rain, and dew, and frost.

Imagine a world that had no water. How different everything would be. Water is part of the way the world works, and all living things depend on it.

But *why* is there water? The 'why' questions are always the hardest! The most famous book in the world, the Bible, says that in the beginning God made the water and the dry land, and then he made all the plants and animals and people to enjoy and care for the world he had made.

One thing is certain: we live in a beautiful world full of amazing designs.

Contents

▶ 1 World of water

When you think of the world, you probably think first of the land.

But people, plants and animals all need water to live.

Our world is made of land and water. Together they provide living things with what they need.

Beginnings of life

You will need:

- two plastic trays lined with kitchen towel
- cress seeds
- water

What to do:

1 Sprinkle your cress seeds over the kitchen towel. Add a little water to one of the trays so the paper towel is moist.

2 Leave the trays in a place that gets some light.

3 Check them every day. Make sure that the towel in the tray you watered stays moist. Add a little extra water when necessary.

4 Watch to see how the seeds grow.

The Wonder of Water

by
Bonita Searle-Barnes

Illustrated by Colin Smithson

A LION BOOK

Text by Bonita Searle-Barnes
Copyright © 1993 Lion
Publishing
Illustrations copyright ©
1993 Colin Smithson

Published by
Lion Publishing plc
Sandy Lane West, Oxford,
England
ISBN 0 7459 2022 5

Albatross Books Pty Ltd
PO Box 320, Sutherland,
NSW 2232, Australia
ISBN 0 7324 0509 2

First edition 1993
10 9 8 7 6 5 4 3 2 1

Acknowledgments
Photographs by Ardea
London Ltd/François
Gohier: spread 11; Lion
Publishing: spread 3 (middle
and bottom); Oxford
Scientific Films/Doug Allan:
spread 14 (left)/Stan
Osolinski: spread 4/Frithjov
Skibbe: spread 9/David
Thompson: spread 5/G.H.
Thompson: spread 10/Barrie
E. Watts: spread 14 (right)/
Kim Westerskov: spread 6;
Nicholas Rous: spread 3 (top);
Harry Smith Horticultural
Photographic Collection:
spread 1; Zefa (UK) Ltd:
cover, spreads 2, 8 (left and
right), 12, 13

A catalogue record for this
book is available
from the British Library

Printed and bound in
Singapore

Water...
and a whole lot
more!

Children love finding out about the world they live in. This book provides loads of activities to help them find out about water. They can have hours of fun watching the way it works and noting their discoveries. In this way they will learn the basic skills of scientific research.

- *More* They can also find out about some of the ways water can be put to work in everyday technology. Exciting projects enable them to discover the fun and the satisfaction of inventing.

- *More* Throughout the ages, children, poets, artists, and some of the world's greatest scientists have thrilled to the wonder of the natural world: the detail, the design, the beauty. The photos in this book are a starting point for discovering more. They encourage children to look for design and beauty in the everyday world around them... dewdrops sparkling like diamonds on a spider's web, clouds drifting in fantastic shapes across the sky, and help them to enjoy their world.

- *More* This book helps them, too, to find words that express the sense of excitement and joy in it all. Here is an opportunity to explore the rich heritage of poems and songs that people have written to celebrate their world. For example, this book draws on the Psalms of the Bible which have echoed the feelings of millions throughout the centuries and which reflect the belief that the world is not the result of chance, but the work of a wise and loving God.

- *More* There is the question, too, of how water makes us feel. Deep, dark waters can be menacing, but clear, sparkling water is cooling and refreshing. Children will talk about these things as they do the different activities. It is a perfect opportunity to reassure them in everyday matters.

- *More* Going beyond the everyday world, you will find natural openings for talking about the symbolic use of water, which they will find in songs and stories and in a good deal of religious language. For example, the Bible speaks of Jesus as the water of life: providing people with what they really thirst for and meeting their deepest needs. Water is used as a symbol in other religions, too. You can talk about the kinds of symbols children see around them, and explain their meaning for those who use them.

This book is intended to give a very broad approach to exploring water, that will enrich your children's total understanding of the world. You'll be surprised at what you discover, too, as you explore the world through a child's eyes.

Water on tap

Think of all the ways you use water in a day. What would life be like if you had no water?

Water to drink

Think about how you feel when you are thirsty. People sometimes use the word thirst about other things, because they want and need them so badly. These lines are from the Bible. What do you think they mean?

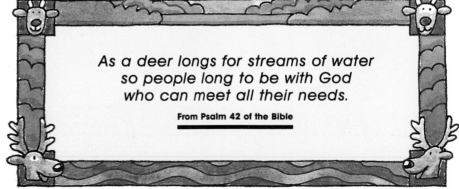

As a deer longs for streams of water so people long to be with God who can meet all their needs.

From Psalm 42 of the Bible

Most of the world's water is found in the oceans and seas.

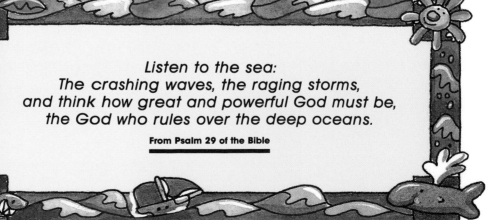

Listen to the sea:
The crashing waves, the raging storms,
and think how great and powerful God must be,
the God who rules over the deep oceans.

From Psalm 29 of the Bible

Salt water

The water in the seas and oceans is salty. You can taste the salt if you happen to swallow any when you go bathing in the sea!

You will need:

- a jug of water
- a spoon
- salt

Aha! I've found it again.

What to do:

1 Put some salt into the water. Can you see the salt as it goes in?

2 Give the water a stir. Can you still see the same amount of salt?

3 Try adding more salt, and stirring it each time you add some more.

   Does it disappear every time?

- Try dipping your finger in the water and licking it. Is the water salty?

- Pour some of your salty water on to a saucer and leave it on a sunny windowsill for a week. What happens to the water?

- Rub your finger over the saucer and lick it. What has happened to the salt?

Tides

If you go down to the shore you will see that the sea is sometimes quite close: the tide is in.

   Sometimes it is far away: the tide is out.

   When the tide comes in, it rushes over everything in its path.

Which of these sandcastles will last the longest when the tide comes in?

▶ 3 Up and away
Puddle brigade

1 Next time it rains, watch where a puddle forms.

2 When it stops raining, mark a line of stones around the puddle.

3 Check your puddle every hour. You will be able to see from your line of stones how much smaller it has become.

● Where is the water going?

● How long did it take for your puddle to disappear?

It's vanished into thin air.

Cloud colours

When the sun shines on the sea, it makes it warmer. This makes some of the water disappear into the air like your puddle did. This invisible form of water is called water vapour.

The vapour rises up into the sky with the warm air. High in the sky it is cold. The water vapour cools again and turns back into water droplets or even into ice, helped by dust in the air. Clouds are made of these tiny specks of water or ice, which are so small and light that they float in the air.

Look up at the sky! Often you will see clouds.

Look at their fantastic shapes.

Look for their different colours. Have you seen...

- fluffy white clouds in a blue sky?
- wispy pink clouds in a morning sky?
- bulging grey clouds in a stormy sky?

What kinds of clouds have you seen?

Why do I always paint clouds white?

▶ 4 Rain and snow

Rain is water that falls from the clouds.

There are millions of tiny water droplets in a cloud. Sometimes they join together in the cloud to make bigger drops.

In the end the drops of water grow too big to float in the air. They fall to the ground.

Rain gauge

Make your own rain gauge, to measure how much rain falls.

You will need:

- an old squeezy bottle
- a pair of scissors
- an old bowl half filled with soil
- a ruler

What to do:

1 Cut the top off the squeezy bottle.

2 Turn the top upside-down and wedge it in the bottom of the squeezy bottle.

3 Stand the bottle upright in the bowl of soil.

4 Stand your rain gauge out in the open, as far away from trees and buildings as you can.

5 Each day, check your rain gauge. Measure how much has fallen in millimetres.

Snowflakes

Hooray for snow! Time for tumbling, sliding, jumping.

When the weather is very cold, the tiny drops of water in clouds may turn to ice. Each piece of ice forms a shape called a crystal. These join together and grow into snowflakes.

Snowflake patterns

Snowflakes have amazingly beautiful patterns, and every single one is different.

I'd like to design some snowflakes too.

I see the work of a Master Designer.

▶ 5 Water on the ground

When it rains, some rainwater flows on top of the land, as streams and rivers. They are channels that let the water flow quickly downhill. Some raindrops sink into the soil.

They will trickle down through the soil.

Some of the water will be taken by the roots of plants. Some will be used by animals that live in the soil.

The rest will travel as far down as it can get.

Underground lake

You will need:

- a sand pit
  or a large bowl of sand
- watering can

What to do:

1 Divide the sand into two areas, with a ridge in the middle.

2 Pour the water from a watering-can into one part only. This is like rain.

3 Leave the other part dry.

4 When the surface of the sand in the half you watered looks dry, dig down below the surface.

5 Now try the other area. Does the sand feel damp when you dig here? Where does the wetness come from?

Hm. The pool must have spread out to the other half.

Flood control

You can make a little river if you dig a channel in soil or sand. The water will flow down it.

From Psalm 18 of the Bible

▶ 6 Water forever

There is a huge supply of water in the seas and oceans.

There is always some of it rising up into the air, where it makes clouds.

The clouds fall as rain.

The rainwater runs over and under the ground, always running downhill.

In the end, it runs back to the seas and oceans.

Bottle world

A bottle garden is a miniature world with its own little water cycle.

You will need:

- a glass bowl or bottle and top
- soil
- small plants or seeds
- a funnel
- several sticks or skewers
- a jug of water

What to do:

1 Put the funnel over the bottle opening and pour in about 2.5cm of soil. Shake it to level it.

2 Use two sticks to hold the plant as you carefully place it in a hole in the soil.

3 Or you can simply scatter seeds over the soil.

4 Gently water the soil. Put the top on. Now

This pattern of water—rising up to make clouds, travelling along in the air, then falling as rain that runs into streams and rivers—never stops.

It is called the water cycle.

The water cycle is part of the world's wonderful design: everything works together to provide all living things with what they need.

I never need to water my bottle garden.

place your bottle garden where it will get lots of light, but not too much hot sun.

• Watch it every day. Where do you see water?

• Where did this water come from?

God cares for the land.
He sends the rain to water it.
It fills the streams
and softens the soil
so the young plants can grow
and give us a rich harvest of food.
The whole world sings with joy.

From Psalm 65 of the Bible

▶ 7 Water for everyone

Have you noticed that water always flows downwards whenever it can?

Because that is how water works, the water that comes out of the taps in your home has to come from somewhere higher up.

Follow the path of the water, from the clean supply to the sewage works where dirty water is cleaned.

- Where is the main supply of water?
- How do you think the water gets upstairs in the house?

Camp shower

Make this outdoors, or try it in the bath!

You will need:

- a large plastic bag
- a knitting needle
- strong string
- a bucket of water
- steps or a stool to stand on

What to do:

1 Use the knitting needle to poke lots of small holes in your plastic bag.

2 Tie the bag up high (or ask a grown-up to hold it for you).

3 Stand on steps to pour the bucket of water into the bag.

4 The shower will begin right away!

Now it flows down to the sea.

► 8 Water power

Look at the water in a waterfall, rushing over a cliff and tumbling down on to the rocks below, knocking any loose pebbles out of the way! Look at the glittering spray, listen to the crashing sounds.

It's wonderful to look at waterfalls because they are so beautiful.

People can also use the power of falling water to do work for them.

Water wheel

You will need:

- the metal foil top from a yoghurt carton
- scissors
- a knitting needle

It turns!

What to do:

1 Push the knitting needle through the centre of the foil, then take it out again.

2 Now make 8 cuts at equal distances around the edge. Twist the pieces between the cuts to make paddles.

3 Push the knitting needle back through the hole, and push the wheel gently to the knob end. Check that the foil turns easily on the needle.

4 Turn on the cold tap to give a gentle stream of water. Hold the foil wheel under it so that the water hits the paddles.

Water mills

Water mills have giant wheels that use the power of running water to turn machinery.

Fast-flowing water is also used to turn special machines that make electricity—the power that makes lights work, and many other machines too. It is a very good way to make electricity, as it uses the natural flow of water and doesn't pollute the earth.

▶9 Heaps of water
Water drops

They're like little round heaps.

Splash a little water on to a smooth, hard surface.

- Look at the shape of the water drops from the top.
- What do they look like from the side? Bend down to get a good look.

Next time you go out for a walk when it has been raining, look at the way water forms drops on different objects. Look at the shape of the drops.

Look at the way the water hangs on this spider's web. It makes little droplets that sparkle and shine in the sunshine like diamonds on a necklace.

Over the top

You will need:

- a glass tumbler
- a jug of water
- a needle or pin

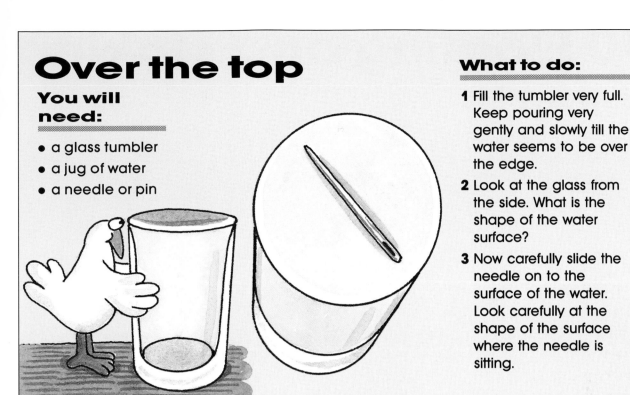

What to do:

1. Fill the tumbler very full. Keep pouring very gently and slowly till the water seems to be over the edge.
2. Look at the glass from the side. What is the shape of the water surface?
3. Now carefully slide the needle on to the surface of the water. Look carefully at the shape of the surface where the needle is sitting.

Holding together

The shape of this group depends on the birds in the outer ring, because they are holding hands. In the same sort of way, the outer part of a drop of water holds together and gives the drop its shape. This holding together is called surface tension.

▶ 10 Floating and sinking

Afloat

Find out what sorts of things sink and what sorts of things float.

1 Collect lots of small objects that won't be spoiled if you put them in water. Here are some to look for:

- coin
- marble
- leaf
- twig
- cork
- stone

2 Drop them into a bowl of water. Which ones sink? Which ones float?

Have a look at a pond or river.

What can you see floating on the surface?

What things sink to the bottom?

Boats

Boats are made with thin walls and a large space in the middle, to be as light as possible. They float well because the water underneath pushes upwards as it tries to get back into the space the boat is in. Although the weight of the boat pushes downwards, the water pushes upwards more, and so the boat floats.

Make your own boat and find out what happens if you make it heavier.

You will need:

- a plastic tub with a flat bottom that floats well
- a pen with waterproof ink
- a bowl of water
- a cargo such as marbles or coins

What to do:

1 Float your tub on the bowl of water like a boat.

2 Notice where the water comes up to. Take the tub out of the water and dry it well, so that you can draw a line on the boat at this point.

3 Now float the boat again.

4 Add some cargo, spreading it evenly over the bottom of the boat. Where does the water come to now?

- How much cargo can you add before the boat sinks?
- What happens if you load the cargo on one side only?

Look for silvery bubbles in clear water.

A bubble is a ball of air surrounded by water.

The plants and animals that live underwater make bubbles when they breathe out air.

You can do this too, if you put your head under the water in a swimming-pool—ask a grown-up to help you, and make sure you are safe.

Rubber bubble, water bubble

You will need:

- a balloon
- string
- a bowl of water

What to do:

1 Blow up the balloon and tie the top with string. It is like a bubble of air with a rubber skin.

2 Try to hold it under the water. Is this easy? What happens if you let it go?

3 Now untie the balloon and hold it closed with your finger.

4 Hold the balloon under the water and open your fingers a little to let the air out. What happens to the air? Where does it go?

Bubble hide-and-seek

You will need:

- a see-through plastic bottle
- water
- a few drops of food colouring

What to do:

1 Fill the bottle almost to the top and add a few drops of food colouring.

2 Put the top on firmly and hold the bottle upside down. Can you see an air bubble? Where is it?

3 Now lay the bottle on its side. Where is the bubble now?

4 Tilt the bottle. Where does the bubble go to?

Water level

Turn your bottle into a handy gadget.

1 Lay it on a flat, level surface, such as a table, and wait till the bubble is still.

2 Draw a line either side of the bubble with a marker pen.

3 Now hold your bottle on other things, such as the top of an armchair, the top of the phone, the banister rail.

4 Look carefully. Does the bubble still rest between the lines? What does it mean if it does? What does it mean if it doesn't?

▶ 12 Frost

Have you ever seen beautiful patterns of frost, decorating the trees and the grasses, and swirling over window panes? Sometimes it makes such wonderful patterns, it looks as if a great artist has been at work.

Frost is made up of tiny bits of ice.

It comes from water in the air, that freezes onto cold surfaces.

That's amazing

Water in the air

You will need:

- a mirror

What to do:

1 Breathe out hard on to a mirror. What happens to the shiny surface?

2 Now breathe on the mirror some more, and run your finger over the surface. What is on your finger? Where did it come from?

Frost in summer

You can make your own frost, even in summer.

You will need:

- a plastic bottle
- water

What to do:

1 Freeze some water in a plastic bottle.

2 When it is solid, take the bottle out of the freezer and wipe it so that it is quite dry.

3 Now leave it in the room for a few minutes. What do you see on the surface of the bottle now?

4 Scrape some off with your fingernail and wait a few moments. What is on your finger now?

▶13 Ice

Icebergs are like great mountains of frozen water. Only the tip of the iceberg shows above the water as they float around in the cold oceans of the world.

Icebergs

You will need:

- ice-cube tray
- see-through bowl
- water

But ice is water—so how can it be heavier or lighter?

What to do:

1 Put some water in an ice-cube tray and freeze it.
2 Then tip your ice cubes into a see-through bowl half filled with cold water.

- Do the ice cubes float?
- Are they mainly above the water or below the water?
- Is ice heavier than water, lighter than water, or the same as water?
- Find out with the next activity.

Escaping ice

You will need:

- a plastic pot with a snap-on lid
- water

It's pushed the lid off.

It needs more room.

What to do:

1 Fill the plastic pot to the brim with water.

2 Now put the lid on, taking care not to spill any water.

3 Put the pot in the freezer.

4 After a few hours, when all the water has turned to ice, lift it out.

Because ice takes up more room than water, a block of ice is just a bit lighter than the same-size block of water. That's why it floats, but with only a tiny bit above water!

▶ 14 Under the ice

How can seals and fish swim in the frozen sea? Find out on this page.

Ice forms on the top of water first.

Underneath there may still be water. That's very important for the plants and animals that live in the icy lakes and seas of the world. Their lives depend on the way ice works.

The top of their home freezes, but underneath there is still water.

Ice cap

Oh! It looked solid, but it was just a thin layer on top.

You will need:

- a plastic bowl
- water

What to do:

1 Put some water in a bowl, and put it in the freezer.

2 Take it out every hour. Has any ice formed? Can you push a hole through the ice?

God sends the winter cold,
the snow, the frost, the hail,
God sends the warm spring wind
that makes the rivers flow again.

From Psalm 147 of the Bible

The good shepherd takes care of his sheep.
He takes them to pools of clear water,
he lets them rest in fields of green grass.
He protects them from danger.
God is my shepherd.
He takes care of me
and gives me everything I need.

From Psalm 23 of the Bible